RARITY OF Beauty

RARITY OF Beauty

ASIA MARIE JACKSON

Afflatus Press Publishing
Thousand Oaks, CA 91359
www.afflatuspresspublishing.webnode.net

Rarity of Beauty
By Asia Marie Jackson

Copyright © 2003 Asia Marie Jackson
ALL RIGHTS RESERVED

First Printing—August 2009
Second Printing- January 2012
ISBN: 978-0985743734

NO PART OF THIS BOOK MAY BE REPRODUCED
IN ANY FORM, BY PHOTOCOPYING OR BY ANY
ELECTRONIC OR MECHANICAL MEANS,
INCLUDING INFORMATION STORAGE OR
RETRIEVAL SYSTEMS, WITHOUT PERMISSION
IN WRITING FROM THE COPYRIGHT OWNER/AUTHOR

Printed in the U.S.A.

Special thanks to all those that have and continue to influence my life.

Contents

Rarity Of Beauty	1
Comforts Me	2
My Edge Of The Sky	3
Rain	4
Get Up Stand	5
Love How	6
Curious	7
Rain Dreams Of He	8
He Says	10
Beyond Reaches	11
I Do Enjoy His Writings	12
My First Impression	14
Reunited Energy	15
Eyes Of Tears	16
My Heart Soars	17
Proud To Be With	18
Bald Eagle Eyes	20
Smile Now Cry Later	21
Lust	22
Can We Talk	24
Listen To Hear	25
Don't Miss The Boat	26

Valley Summer	27
Sitting On A Bench At The Park	28
Music To My Ears	29
Accompany Me	30
Not Anymore	31
My Apology	32
Ocean Views	33
Consequence Bigger Than Risk	34
Lava Explodes	35
Who's Counting?	36
You Need Prepare	37
Grounded	38
Beyond Soul	39
Fly On The Wall	40
Twelve Roses Long	41
Day And Night Glares	42
Naturally	43
The Unborn	44
In God We Trust	45
Thank You Mother For Your Prayers	46
Mothers Love	47
Black Mother	49
Don't Fear Change	54
Required?	55
King Of Love	56

Styles. Of. All. Kinds	57
Nadia Inspired	58
Withholding	59
Uninvited	60
Unsettled	62
Tha' Eight Wonder	63
She-She	64
Dish	65
As One	66
Tango For Two	67
To Settle	68
Good Violence	69
Contradiction	70
Remember Me	71
Oh So Magnetic	72
Prove It	74
Random Thinking	76
Forbidden Fruit	78
Shh ...	79
Mi Casa Es Su Casa	80
Making Up Feel So Good	81
Instinct Reacts	82
Poetic Intercourse	84
Letting Go	85
Reality	86

Mind Games	87
Reflection	88
A Beauty Disaster	89
Blind My Eyes So I Can Love	90
Advice To Young Loves	91
Defined By rules	92
Shades Faces	93
Power Play	94
Blind Is Love	96
Unscramble Me	97
Mind Gamez	98
Does He Know Him?	99
Grey Hound Bus	100
There Is No End	101
Israel	102
Routine	103
Dear Tonka	104
Who Am I?	106
Scorpio	107
Frame Of Mind	108
Fluttering Beauty	109
God Made Me Free	111
Me Being Me	113

ACKNOWLEDGEMENTS

I would like to express my appreciation,

To my son, Travion Marquies McGowan, for your unconditional love, strength, patience and making my life complete (You're amazing!).

To my mother, Oranjarie Brown, for your inspiration, love, prayers, guidance, support, and for sharing your godly wisdom with me. Also for your contribution of three poems.

To my father, Willie Ray Jackson, for exposing me to art, and for all that you are and are not.

To my elder sister, Darlene, for being a positive-motivating influence in my life, for your support, for urging me to speak and express myself freely and for always keeping it authentic.

To my elder brother André, for your confidence in me, motivation, and not allowing me to procrastinate.

To my younger brother Kevin, for your trust, encouragement and for believing in me and being my biggest promoter.

To my sister in-law, Kathleen Jackson, for lending me your ear, advice and spiritual support.

To my nephews and niece, André Jr., De'Onzae, and Deja, for your joy, laughter, and love.

To my dear friend Al-Nisa Johnson, for your devotion, for always giving me and my family your support, and for introducing me to the wonderful world of travel.

And finally to my precious family and friends, that have taken an interest in my writing and gave their encouragement: Ronnell Perkins, Lamont Devault, Paula Slaughter, Kimberley Spencer, and Tony Seybert.

Rarity Of Beauty

How can something so priceless and rare

Not be valued for its exquisiteness?

And to add insult to injury

Be replaced

By some modern-day replica of the original?

How could one be so blind

To a beauty that is much deeper than skin?

What happened to good taste?

Acquired? I think not.

Upon its immediate presence,

Its incalculable worth

Is seen, felt, heard and shown.

Compared? Not even close.

To its depth

Its weight

Its design

Its worth.

Its wears and tears accents its charm.

How did the beholder lose the eye for the

Rarity of beauty?

COMFORTS ME

The splendor of love
The softness of the climate
The fragrance of the trees
Comforts Me

The laughter of men
The laughter of women
The laughter of children
Comforts Me

The jazz of a song
The murmur of nature
The brush of the breeze
Comforts Me

The devotion in faith
The power of prayer
The love of God
Comforts Me

The summit of the hills
The thunder of the night
The rhythm of the sea
Comforts Me

My Purpose In Life

For every obstacle there's a positive aspect.

Determination begins

Within the heart and mind.

Find a person with aspiration

And you've found a friend for a lifetime.

Butterflies pollinate plants;

Harp seals play in the snow;

Plant seeds and a tree baring fruit will grow;

Seas belong where they can saunter;

Ravens belong where they can fly.

I've got to be where my spirit can dance free.

Got to find my purpose in life.

Every person has their fantasy;

Every person has their goals.

Faith has a way of attaching to the soul;

Lions have their roar;

Birds have their songs;

Life is meant to be more than just long.

Dolphins belong where they can swim;

Eagles belong where they can soar high;

I've got to be where my spirit can dance free.

Got to find my purpose in life.

Rain

Lord, send the rain
After the withered things are restored
And made green again
The flowers flourish and lend their
Fragrance to the air
Removing the stench of previous despair
Dreams are renewed
Hope is revived
And again we are determined
To give life our hardest try
The rain washes away pain
Allowing us to breathe again
After the rain the dark clouds disappear
And our minds are made miraculously clear
Lord send the rain
We need the rain

By, Orange Arie

GET UP - STAND

Get up - Stand
The time has come
For you to face your fears
Awaken from your mentality
Create your awareness
You can change your reality

Get up - Stand
The time has come
For you to meditate
Whisper to your spirit
And it will hear your authority

Get up - Stand
The time has come
For you to ignite that spark within you
Your life can be renewed

Get up - Stand
The time has come
For you to make a choice
To rule your destiny
Or let nature run its course

LOVE HOW

If you want someone to love you
Never be the same
Allow them into your heart
Not your brain
So if they ache your heart
You'll remain sane
&
If you love someone
Show it from the start
Know it in your mind
Speak it from your heart

CURIOUS

A wondering mind

Seems to wonder itself

Into a deep imaginary sleep

Dreaming of an idealistic world

Escaping reality

To feed its curiosity of what lies

Beneath satin of silk blend sheets

When curiosity and reality meet

Will it be as good as the dream?

Or will it cause feelings of regret

For turning an illusion into something real?

Rain Dreams Of He

Looking out my French windows
Watching the rain fall
I want you next to me so
I contemplate on giving you a call
I choose to see and hear
The rain hit against the glass alone
As hail hits the ground to melt into a puddle
I imagine you here with me in a cuddle
The thunder of the night roars as a King Lion
And since I rule my dreams
Next to me you are lying
Feeling hot from your heat
I imagine
The lightning strikes the dark to spark
A flame of burning desired toes
Playing footsies with bare feet
As I giggle
From the Eskimo kiss I received on the nose
Staring into the rain as if hypnotized
I continue to feel clear skies
When I look into your beautiful eyes
Inhaling the fresh scent of clean
I wonder if you really know what I mean
When I hold you tight throughout the night

Gripping you tighter as the temperature
Grows colder
I dream of my head
Placed upon your shoulder
I imagine
My inner moisture is beyond my control
Yet placing you in my dreams
Gives my dreams a soul

HE SAYS ...

He says ...
I'm his choc·o·lat·ey treat
Sweet enough to eat
Like peaches and cream
I'm the toffee sweetheart he had envisioned
He says ...
I'm a rose
From my onyx tresses
Almond eyes
Persimmon lips
Mahogany skin
To my cinnamon bronze toes
He says ...
I'm the heart of his throne
The most precious jewel his eyes have known
He says ...
My kisses drunken him like fine wine
Divinely picked like grapes off a vine
He says ...
He'll rest with me at sundown
Beneath a tall ebony tree
While the sky turns as dark ... as me

Beyond Reaches

Inside the deepest segment

Of our hearts

Are cravings

We dare not mention.

So intense

So exhilarating

So extravagant

So invigorating

So enigmatic

So fervent

So passionate

Our most private crazes glistens

At the essence of our being

Alluring us to the heights of bliss

And depths of despair.

I tried to express my own desires

And urged you to abandon yourself with me.

I only wanted your heart.

Now that that's gone,

You have nothing more to offer.

I Do Enjoy His Writing

I'm his favorite prose.

In his poetry

Every line of me

Heightens his suspense.

He's addicted and can't let go of me

I'm his drug

His ultimate high.

He floats as he rips off my silk line

He uses metaphors to bind me

I'm hypnotized

He's in my mind

I'm etched in his written text

Chained to his intellect

I'm his written trophy

Attached to his philosophy.

I'm his strong highly flavored sweet liqueur

After a few shots of me

Illusion and reality equally occur

Acting out images from his brilliant mind

Inhaling my ink

While he consumes my eloquence

Expunging my innocence

Writing in his deepest syllables

Climaxing his phrase

Drowning me with his passionate overdose
Using his eyes to read me like a poetic verse
Bringing out the best in me.
In his couplet we luxuriate
Sensually, mentally
Physically and emotionally
Satiate …
Mutually.
I do enjoy his writing

My First Impression

He sent my heart hovering
On the satin ribbon of his approach
His fanatical kiss
Scorched my lips
And moistened the inside of my hips
When I gazed on him
For a moment
My heartbeat became rapid
My breath became thick
My voice fell soundless
And a subtle flame
Burned underneath my skin
My heart was on fire
I felt my entire body softening
Quivering like a ascending lambent of
Fragile flames
Melting me inside
My qualms were freed
My knees weakened
And my legs fatigued
From a night of cloud dancing

Reunited Energy

When our vibes met
It wasn't coincidence
We were instantly drawn to each other's eyes
Without ruse nor disguise
An energy elapsed between us
Unmasking this unique passion
Burning deep inside us.
The way you smiled at me as I looked up
How could a smile have said so much?
And cause such a sensation without a touch?
A chemistry
That made two people who have never met
Feel so connected
On that day our souls merged
As we stared into each others eyes
Presumably losing our measure of time.
I must have known you in another lifetime
That would explain how you reached my core
Ooh … what we must have shared
What we must have done in our lives before
We must have loved each other in the past
Our souls reunite at last

Eyes Of Tears

Regretful feelings

Heartaches of wishes

To turn back the clock.

Even if the watch stood still

Time will never comply.

Whys

Haunt the mind.

What ifs

Taunt the soul.

Like a continuous covey

Of unanswered questions:

Maybe a pause is the answer.

Unwind thinking before action takes place.

Is the reason

Reason enough?

Tears flow in a puddle of regret.

My Heart Soars

Darkness surrounds me

As my eyes open and focus

I notice

A glowing red glare

Shaped like a C on the left side

And a backward C on the right

It's the only thing giving this place light

There is sound

I hear a sound

Pound, pound, pound (repeatedly)

My heart soars

Proud To Be With

What we share is
Beautiful love
Contagious love
Genuine never forged love
Love you whenever, wherever, however,
Who-cares-what-they-think kind of love
Calm never hostile love
Suitable for us because we're happily in love
Not counterfeit love nor imitation love
Flirtatious, enticing, alluring love
Charming, appealing, engaging-type shit
Factual, honorable, and proud to be with,
Down on bended knee, this is it! love
Demonstrative, conversational
And inspirational love
Spoken love
Feeling right in my soul love
Together forever for better or worse love
Through goodness and in health,
Until death do us part-type shit
Trusting, honest, and proud to be with,
Bold and energetic love
Spirited, brave and lively love
Not pretentious love

Quiet love

Mess with my love, cause a riot-type shit

Supply, provide, and proud to be with,

Feel to die if I lost you love

Exist in your heart for life love

Mystical-type shit

Wearing my heart on my sleeve,

Tell the world you're mine

Surreal feel,

Real and offered love

When God made you he broke the seal love

One of a kind love

Ideal love

Complete and concrete-type shit

Forget understanding,

Just accepting it love

Smiling love

Shining love

Singin' in the rain-type shit

Faithful, loyal and proud to be with

BALD EAGLE EYES

Soaring on top of it all ... lurking eyes
Looks within
As it flies above
In unison ... with the wind
It judges
Within ... and ... outside
A language it cannot understand
A way of life it is unfamiliar with
Mammals of different textured skin
Yet it squawks
In attempt ... of communicating
With mouth moving mutes
Receiving a response
Not relating
To the pea size of its brain

Smile Now Cry Later

Sometimes I cry
When the lights go dim
I can't help but to reminisce
On hurtful past events
The world is in rotation
Before I could never tell
But ones have come and gone so fast
I'm dizzy from their spin
A lost ark set to sail
A treasure not lost until found
Once its place is taken,
No one stays around
Again the sun must set
And lights again go dim
And again I cry
In reminisce
Of
Hurtful past events

LUST

Lust
Excessive
Sexual
Desires

Lust
Highly ... gratifying
To taste
To hear
To see
To smell
To touch

Lust
Delighting
All of your senses

Lust
Glowing ... through
A
Lurid
Haze
As
Flames ... enveloped

Lust

Like … smoke

It

Lingers … in air

Until … you

Toke

In

A

Gust of me

Then … hold

Me

In

Until … I

Reach

Your … brain

Lust

Relaxing your senses

Insane … feeling

So … good

CAN WE TALK?

I liked it when I could talk to you
And you could talk to me
And if we disagreed,
Well … that was just going to be.
Tell me
When did we take that transition
To stop understanding one another
And start disrespecting each other?
Is it that we love one another so much
That we hate each other?
I now realize
Why it's a thin line between love and hate
Because they're not totally opposite
Neither is fate and you and I.
So
Why are we letting go something great?

LISTEN TO HEAR

Let the music from strings on guitars
Bring you far
Into the stars of my eyes
Let songs from beautiful birds
Guide you to glide inside my mind where
Love and compassion reside
Seek deeper then the heart of my heat
Into my soul that carry rhythms
That will make your feet tap to its beat
That pound so loud
It makes people wonder
How?
And is she the golden child?
As that sit for a while and marinates
Let the whisper of words of the greats
Blow into your ears to elevate your mind state
Like the sound a piano make
When combined with ebony and ivory keys
If we are made for this world
Then the world and we can relate
And we agree ... that we should be
As free as the sound of music

DON'T MISS THE BOAT

I need a vacation and relaxation
Send me to the right destination
Where I will feel more at ease
I will finally breathe

At times
My mind
Makes me feel like
A feline baptized with
Lime of tequila and sunrise

Those that surround themselves with no escape
Find themselves empty

Wondering about the
Feline whom is baptized with
Sunrise tequila and lime

Always wondering if they have missed their time
To open up and unwind

Valley Summer

The day is hot ... boiling hot!

My face is oily

My sun block is shinning

My skin is frying

My eyes are squint

My feet feel swollen

The sun is breathing down my neck

My lipstick is dripping

My makeup is smudging

My water is warm and I just paid for it!

My breast is sweaty

My hands are clamming

My heart is pumping

And

I'm craving ice cream

Cool isn't it?

I love the valley

Even in the heat!

SITING ON THE BENCH AT THE PARK

He look in her eyes
She smiles
And bashfully look away
As if she's too shy to allow their stare
To turn into a kiss
Even though she want it so badly
He rubs her braided hair
She fiddles with her hands underneath the bench
So that he could not see her nervousness
He reaches to hold her hand
Her foot began to shake
She smiles
He says something to make her laugh
While tilting her head back in laughter
He look her in the eyes
Down to her neck
And tells her how beautiful she is
Closing her eyes to accept his kiss
As she did his compliment
Feeling every bit of pretty as he sees her

Music To My Ears

Opera
The greatest grace that can ever be given
A beauty of form that comes deep from within
Music to my ears
How beautiful the sound
That soothes my soul
My body's in tuned with each tone
Such elegance
Such grace
So extraordinary and peaceful
Yet powerful and meaningful
Music to my ears
How sweet the sound
So mysterious
Yet serious
It captures my soul
Pleasing my senses taking a calming control
Guiding my imagination to run wild
Highly respected
Standing ovations accompany applause
Bravo!

ACCOMPANY ME

With you, I am pleased
I admire your dignity, your personality
Your gallantry, your style,
Your mentality, your smile
And the security you give me.

Will you accompany me
For a stroll along the shore
So our feet can be cleansed by the sea?

Will you accompany me to a place
Where we're surrounded in ecstasy
Lost between wrong and right
Caught between dark and light?

Will you accompany me to a place
Where we'll hear nothing and everything
Become speechless yet heard
Noticed but unseen?

Will you accompany me to a place
Where our spirits can roam deeply
Somewhere we can be free?

NOT ANYMORE

She never had a first love
Only a past
Of being manipulated
For one's own advantage
Their disguise could not be recognized
It's hard distinguishing truth from lies
When blue covers the sky
And love is thought to be blind
As her soul soars to new destinations
Her destiny flies in gyration
Her imagination
Was the true instigation
For making an illusion
Seem so realistic
Rationalizing confusion
Is all in the past.
She's content within
Opening her perception
Becoming more intuitive
To the way she lives
And
To the people she allows in her realm

MY APOLOGIES

I would like to apologize to the man ... I
Left heart feeling burglarized ... but ... I
Could no longer visualize ... us
Staying together after ... I
Realized you were wearing a disguise ... by
Feeding me lies ... and
Behaving uncivilized ... I
Could no longer agonize myself ... in
This familiarized chastise
Many times ... I
Tried to analyze ... my
Hypnotized feelings
Every time your eyes ... and ... my
Unauthorized thoughts of denies
Jeopardized ... my
Harmonized compromise ... I
Hate to criticize ... but ... it's
No surprise ... our
Skies were gray even at sunrise
Otherwise ... we
Would still be together ... my
Apologies

OCEAN VIEWS

The time is 6 p.m. Pacific Coast time

I'm at the beach
Just where the ocean begins and the shore ends
My feet is sunk in the sand
And covered by the oceans body at once.

I'm at the beach
Just where the ocean begins and the shore ends
Looking over this massive body of
Controlled warmth
Its infinite beauty and harmonious motion
Have me in a state of hypnotic
As if under a spell
I am mesmerized
By its ability to mirror hues
Of black, green and blue
The mystery of its deep layers
Keeps in suspense of its hidden treasures.

I'm at the beach
Just where the ocean begins and the shore ends
Looking over this obedient body of
Magnificence
Feeling so blessed to witness
God's dominance.

CONSEQUENCE BIGGER THAN RISK

Although like and dislike
Comes to mind when thinking of you
There is something holding
My curiosity and attention toward you
What I know ... should be enough
For me to give my thoughts up
Curiosity may kill my emotions
But if I don't research your soul
My emotions may be put temporarily on hold
At least I'll know what I already knew
Even though I wish I had not
It's that something
My finger can't quite put a hold on
Yet everything wrong is staring me in the face
It isn't to change just to understand the strange
And the unidentified cause
That keeps me in suspense
Of what will make of this.
If I reap the repercussion
Will I learn from my mistake?
Or will I
Continue to search behind another unknown face?
Whichever the case ... I'll never dismiss
Taking on a risk with a bigger consequence.

Lava Explodes

The volcano within me
Erupts with time
One with my inside
Melting my mind
Lava soars through each part of me
You see my cool outer layer
While my insides a' steaming
As tight as my lips are sealed
Instantaneously
My mind shoots fiery thoughts
So flaming hot
I think aloud!

Who's Counting?

What's behind this feeling I feel?
I mean
Worthwhile it seems
My clouded reflection eyes me like a bird of prey
The profile of his night
Slanted by the light of his day
But if he walks away
His name will remain on my walls
Feelings weak to fall
When his strong eyes look through mine
I'm a window clear to shine
Although I have thoughts of his tongue running
Up-down down and up my spine
I believe his the one for me
He can make me his vessel if we could agree
The top and bottom diameter define
To bear that proportion as six to nine
No less
No more
In the depths of the prominent I'll explore
Along a new love has crossed my path
But will it last?
You do the math

You Need Prepare

You are on a road to a broken heart
Some of life's simple things have yet to start
I am taking control
I tried not to be unkind
But if I stay with you
I'll lose my mind
It is just a waste of our time
You need prepare
I must confess
In my life experiences
You have played a major part
It now seems as if
I've lost an oblivious friend.
I think it would be best
If I returned to the West Coast
And you remained on the South Coast
You need prepare
I will always love you because
You have influenced my life
But I no longer wish to be your wife

Grounded

Don't be fooled by smiles

For they often hide sorrow

Don't be misled by words

For they often speak of lies

Don't be blinded by eyes

For they don't lie but will deceive

Don't allow a hug to hold you

For your feet are well capable

Beyond Soul

A soul captured in a body of water
Thoughts floating in a sea of waves
Sinking deep into the brain
Words and thoughts are rearranging
Tides of judgments are all disappearing
Oceans of faith are all reappearing
The water is twisting and turning all around
It's spinning in every direction breaking ground
Right before I subside
Something grabs me from within
My eyes widen my body's soaking wet
I'm caught between reality and illusion
Screaming so loud that my throat swells up
Trying to move but I can't get up
Realizing I rule my destiny
As I'm drowning in my soul
My arms become numb
My body is cold
As I awaken reality becomes real
Life has a purpose my soul is healed
Life begins

FLY ON THE WALL

He acts as if she does not exist
As if she is a fly on the wall that he cannot see
Yet in reality … she is just being she
Oh-so-aloof is his vibe
So unaware that she is near
Ignoring her significance
He is either ashamed or he fears
What people may say
The whispers
The snickers
When he is with her day after day
He assumes that she does not mind
Because she tend to hide her feelings inside
Then … she whispers it
Three little words that carries such a huge impact
Then … she … awaits
He shun her in silence
By the time he responded
It was too late
Now … she acts as if he does not exist
As if he is a fly on the wall that she cannot see
Yet in reality... she is just being she

TWELVE ROSES LONG

A dozen roses
One for each day
After the twelfth
You distant yourself
You're not up for the chase
The excuse you use
But who's giving you a race?
On my face, in my eyes and by my touch
You knew I would miss you much
But lack of respect and lust
Made you not give a fuck
So as I watch the roses rot
In the clear crystal vase
I will forget you not
Like the roses dropped dead and brittle
Taking on darker hue
It symbolizes my feelings toward you

Day And Night Glares

As the sun slowly glares red
The branches uniquely still
Placed above the trees stem
Perfectly serving its purpose
The tree wouldn't be as beautiful
If it wasn't for them on its surface
Although the leaves appear to be dead
The tree is very much alive
As the day pass to the afternoon
The afternoon will pass to evening
And as the evening pass to night
The darkness becomes light
The dawn with its mist
The day with its sun kiss
The night with its bright stars
The grass with its morning dew
Birds chirping I love you hymns
The morning shines of humanity
And beautiful things like
Blooming roses and violets
While the night remains calm and silent

NATURALLY

My love is merely but a forest
Where thy may roam about freely
Drink from my tributary
And consume my fruits as thy will

The Unborn

Nine months

Then labor with pains

Until the infant

Can bare a brain with brains

The ocean darkens

Now

Visualize black fears

Invisible pains

Lashes cascades of black tears

Demented psychopathic

Dilutes the intellect

The practice is perplex

The surface is planet earth

From birth

We were born to understand

That the woman was designed for the man

IN GOD WE TRUST

It's funny how

When I'm happy … you're ecstatic

When I smile … you're beaming

When I giggle … you're laughing

When I cry … you shed tears

When I'm in pain … you ache

When I'm mad … you're pissed!

Your hand and my hand
Held together forms a fist
Strong we stand together
Because we respect, love, trust and honor God together

Thank You Mother For Your Prayers

I watched you strive
I heard your plea
For God to watch over me.
I saw you on bended knees
Crying out to the Lord our savor
Praying that he excuse my misbehavior
Alike Him you showed me unconditional love
And now I thank God
For helping you to teach me the right way
For you knew I would grow up
To be a woman some day
You prayed in advance for my soul to be saved
And that he touch my body and take away my pain.
So during my life's journey
The roads will be paved
And I would have strength to endure
Through sunshine and rain
Now through your example
I pray the same prayer for my family
Thank you mother for your prayers

MOTHERS LOVE

Your love is profound
It's made of pure allegiance
And of sacrifice and glee
It is infinite, unselfish and enduring
It is patient and forgiving
When all others are forsaking
It never neglects or hesitates
It believes beyond believing
When the world around condemns
It glows with all the beauty
Of the rarest and brightest gems
It is far beyond defining
It defies all explanation
Like the mysteries of creation
A magnificence
A phenomenon
And another wondrous evidence
Of a mothers love and endearment

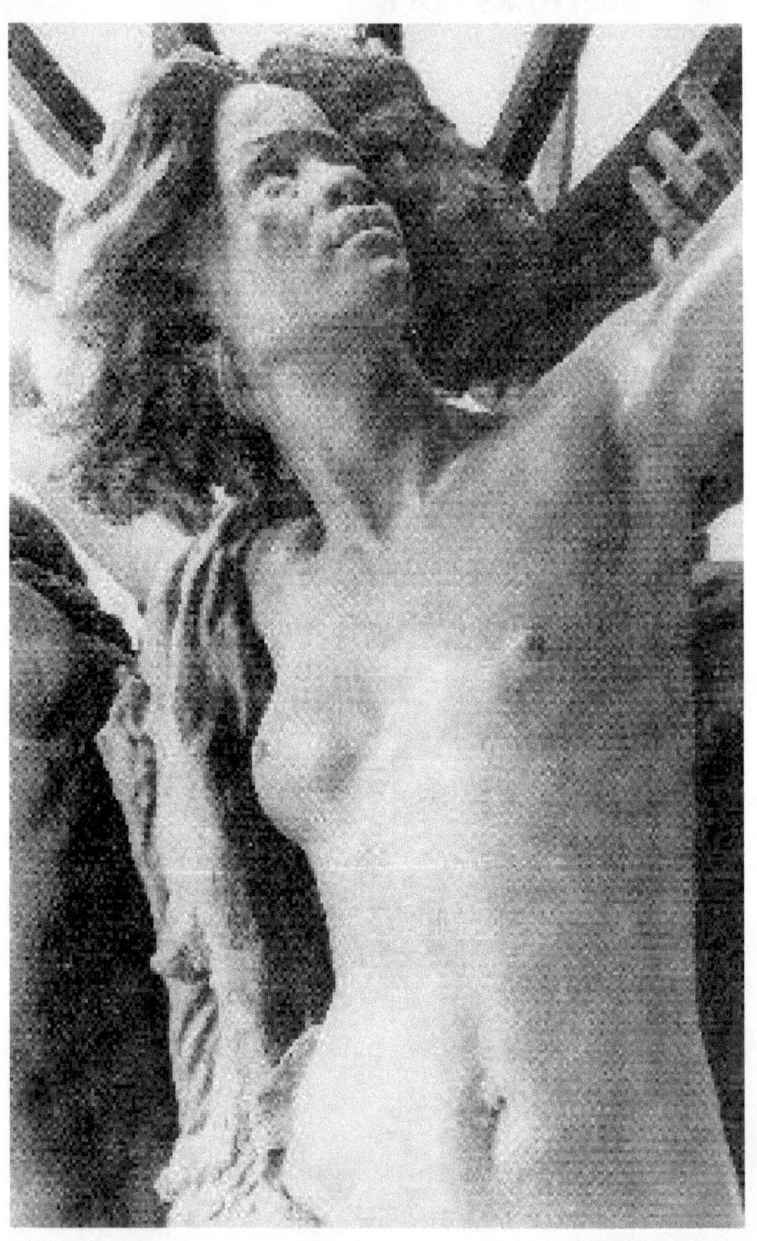

The "Fountain of the Observatory" sculpture by Jean-Baptiste Carpeaux. This picture is of "Africa" one of the four figures of the sculpture Located in Paris, France

BLACK MOTHER

Black Mother, Black Mother
I see you in your kitchen
Oven on
Dishwasher hot
Mop bucket full
Washing machine wringing
And you are walking around singing
You are such a busy bee!
If anyone should ask why
What would be your reply?

I would just say
I'm acting as the maid
Until the maid shows up
And she has not showed up in forty years
And I'm only forty-two

Black Mother, Black Mother
You're walking down the street
At 7:30 a.m. in the morning
With four little children
As happy as can be
Their coats look new
And their boots do too
But Black Mother

Your dress seems rather worn
And your sweater is wearing thin
Why are you out so early
In this cold and gusty wind?

I'm walking my children to school
My car broke down a year ago
And these streets are dangerous, you know
So right now
I'm their security
Until they're old enough to know

Black Mother, Black Mother
I see you in a home
But for some unknown reason
The address is not your own
Furniture polish beside you
Dutch cleanser in one hand
And glass cleaner in the other
Can you give me an explanation
For all of this Black Mother?

Well daughters need shoes
Sons want a bike
I'm a little late with the rent
And the landlord can be such a fright
Since I cannot accept defeat
I'm just being the one that make ends meet

Black Mother, Black Mother
Such a touching sight I see
There's a beautiful black child
With her head upon your knee
Your words are spoken softly
As you stroke her long black hair
Will you tell me Black Mother
The reason her head is there?

My child has a problem
As children often do
But I'm not the type of mother
Who cries "Oh what am I to do?"
So I quickly turn myself into a sponge
That absorbs her growing pains
Her disappointments and her tears
In return I give encouragement
That will last throughout her years

Black Mother, Black Mother
Where are you rushing to?
Your eyes are sad
Your face is tight
Your hands are sweating so
Tell me Black Mother quickly
Where is this place you go?

I'm going to see my son
He's serving time, you know
He had to learn the hard way
Being in the wrong place
At the wrong time
And doing the wrong thing
Will send you to places
You never intended to go
So you see this day is rather new to me
Because today I'm something
I'd thought I'd never be
A visitor with a time limit
Between my child and me

Black Mother, Black Mother
You stand so proud today
With a sparkle in your eyes
A smile kissed by the sun
And you're giving words of encouragement
To each and everyone
Being an observer of all the things you do
I can't help but wonder
What has caused this reaction in you?

My girls are all grown up now
With good jobs and families of their own
They let my son come out that iron gate

The Lord blessed him with a good mind
And now he's living straight
He's at the right place
At the right time
Doing the right thing
And that would cause
Any mother's heart to sing

Black Mother, Black Mother
You're full of years by now
Your eyes are dim, your hair is thin
And your steps are getting slow
But there is one more question
I need to ask and then I'll let you go
Through all these years you have been
Strength, hope and encouragement
To everyone you know
Now I would like to know the source
That caused all these virtues inside of you to grow?

Oh shucks that's easy
I could have answered that question
A long, long time ago
You see I am God's prize possession
And it is He that has made me so

By, Orange Arie

Don't Fear Change

A torn shadow dances on the wall
A girl
A dim semi-empty room
A burning fireplace
A stereo
A Persian rug
A wooden chair she sits on
A lit cigarette
At a brief moment at the end of it all
A decision has to be made
The instant the cigarette has ended
The smoke lingers in air
Similar to her thoughts
While her heart lies on the floor
Quietly among the broken ashes
Her future dances with the flames
Bizarrely blending with
The jazzy music playing
Becoming more content
As she reaches
Another turning point
As destined

REQUIRED?

Pretending not to see the insanity around me

While playing deaf ignoring the sound of my fear.

Am I

Required to be cheerful when I'm not in danger?

Or am I

Required to be cheerless when I'm in anger?

Am I

Required to hold my head down

While the masses pass me by?

Or am I

Required to hold my head up

As I pass among the masses?

Am I

Required to hold back my tears?

Or am I

Required to sit and cry?

Am I

Required to laugh when I fall?

Or am I

Required to stand tall in the mist of it all?

To what do you require?

KING OF LOVE

A vision in a poets dream

Basking in beauty

Thou it seem

An angel robed in spotless white

When the birds sing at night

Release doves

For our love

So that they may fly over me and

My King of love

STYLES. OF. ALL. KINDS

Why is starting a business so hard?

Trademarks, copyrights and business cards

Graphic designs and reading between lines

Utilizing and making the best of my time

I have people to see and investors to kind

But I have yet to find the right people

To fit my u-neek physique

It's just not the time to think twice

I find myself hearing, receiving

And giving the same advice

To read fine lines and to keep my eyes open

On those who are the furthest

And on those who are the closest

Because there will always be that person

Scooping and hoping to undermine you

And me what ever it takes to succeed

I believe my business will be

As long as I keep faith,

Work hard, be patient and never give up

No matter how long it takes

To achieve the success I deserve.

Nadia Insipred

Give her drugs
Get her high
All she wants to do is fly
Taking drugs to get her by
Living in a masquerade
Look at all the friends she has made
This is how the game is played
You know the scars will never fade
Running with the shadows of the night
The lonely darkness eclipses the light
The vision is always black and white
A purple haze distorts her sight
Locked inside her hollow shell
Her life has been a living hell
Look around her empty cell
But what you see you can not tell
Soft-less whispers echoes in her mind
The roads she have traveled were never kind
How could she have been so blind?
The things she has lost
She'll never find

WITHHOLDING

My tears would fall
If they could face my eyes to form
The loads I bare within
Leaves my peace torn
Quiet as kept
Loudly my ears hear my fears
By my lips secrecy is sworn
So I use my head to take mental notes
Off my thoughts to lead
Coming cheek to cheek
And face to face
With a nose that bleeds

UNIVITED

Unannounced you park up at my yard

You ring my doorbell

You knock my door

You tap my windows

And constantly shout my name

Didn't you read the sign posted outside my door?

No visitors!

You bring with you

A right hand filled with six long stem red roses

A left hand filled with three long stem pink roses

And three long stem white roses

Together there's a dozen

You speak spoken words of

I love you

Forgive me

I need you

And

I'm sorry

Is that all that you can say?

Didn't you read the sign posted outside my door?

No soliciting!

Now you know my thoughts

My feelings

My need

What's in my best interest

My wants

And what I should do

So why should I answer you?

Unsettled

The needy turned out to be the lonely
Tête-à-tête
Construct
Blind fold
Covet to live out dialogue
We spoke impromptu lines
Finding commonalities
Creating illusion
We're connected
We're compatible
Satisfying a void
That was left vacant
Without proper notice
Scanning over references
Filling in lines
Desirable to read
Neglecting facts
That soon … HITS
You … SMACK … in the face
Tête-à-tête
Construct
Unmasking … blind fold

Tha' Eighth Wonder

My skin tone glistens like dark liquor
The eighth wonder of the world
A picture perfect pose of a black body
Plump and round shades of black and brown.
Black is beautiful, original and organic
Black is the sexy that mixes
His blood like a hot toddy
Visions in his mind are steamy and naughty
Mixed with nature's rarest juices
A sista's cocktail that produces
The sweet taste of nectar honey.
Senses of my tasty rind is like a vintage fine wine
The essence of a black woman's hourglass
Is the visualization of an expensive sculpture
Naturally fine with shapes and curves
History brings him to the status of a connoisseur
His eyes reflect his favorite addiction
Mother Earth's sweetest piece of fruit on the tree
That take his imagination far beyond the sea.
The eighth wonder of the world
Unfurls the master's plan of a creation so pure.

SHE – SHE

You fell in love

Before ever laying eyes on she

Her voice

Her speech

Her laugh

Her individuality

She is unique

And she has this mysterious mystic

She is impressionable genuine

With she you feel free

Her love

Must be

One in a million

Even with your strong discipline and opinions

You could not conceal

The love you feel within for she

Let down your shield not your guard

Why is excepting, respecting and loving

She for she so hard?

Dish

Mounds of enduring pleasure

His pleasing touch makes me vulnerable

I'm open to his substantial desires

I am his craving

His hunger

His thirst

Best served humid

He is my habit I dare not quit

My drug

My cure

My remedy

My appetite

Best served solid

Together we make quite a dish

As One

Tears drop down the cheek of a face
That has realized its mistake
Everyone has flaws
To except them is loves law
Us together
Is like a handwritten love letter
That seems only to get better and better
With time
As we read over every line of one another
Beautiful memories
Places a smile on our face
And pleasant thoughts of each other
Lingers in our mind
Leaving us proud
That we share our lives together
As one

Tango For Two

The list ... we can go on

To the lunacy that added on

The love triangle, the pain, the anger

The vicious cycle

What happened to it takes two to tango?

If you could feel her pain

You'd feel your soul burn with every thought

There's a scar that may be stitched

But never healed

Trust and love is now something hard to feel

Now that it's been stripped of its true meaning

Just one more excuse for self-beating.

To this life lesson she will always wonder:

For what reason?

Was it something she said?

Was it something unsaid?

Questions will always come up

All she could do is cry

In every moment

Caught in the thought

Just one more part of her dies.

To Settle

A lonely soul controls

Beauty in the eye of its beholder

Leaning to find a shoulder

To break its fall

Vision blurred

By a misunderstanding

Of what has occurred

The soul questions

Which way is up

And which contents to fill her cup

GOOD VIOLENCE

There are always those
That will take
Advantage
Of
The
Weak and non-violent

If it weren't for good violence
The bad violence
Would rule the world

"Proclaim liberty throughout all the land unto all the inhabitants thereof" (Lev. 25:10).

CONTRADICTION

I miss you

Yet I never want to see you

I love your voice

Yet I hate listening to you

I miss talking to you

Yet I don't return your calls

I hate to see you leave

Yet I love to watch you go

I want to be your wife

Yet I'm not one to commit

I'm not in love with you

Yet I say it

I want to pass the test

Yet I never study

I want a good-looking companion

Yet I only date the ugly

I need to spend every moment with you

Yet I can't find the time

I call this a poem

Yet it doesn't even rhyme

Remember Me

Today like everyday way gray

My blue skies and white clouds

Were taking away

No longer does my hair

Blow freely in the wind

Like a snake shedding its skin

A new life for me had to begin

Now I can only remember when

You were my man

My future

My companion

My provider

My protector

My right hand

It came to a mutual end of course

Likewise I'm sure

Oh So Magnetic

With your extraordinary ability to attract
I'm drawn
The intensity between us
Is strong
Your kiss numbs areas of my body
You're anesthetic
We're trapped inside a poetic verse
Oh so magnetic
Creaming the cream of dreams
Pleasing each other
With motion filled
Strokes, moans and screams
Scratches, squeezes and stares
What a sexy scene
Two lovers making steaming love
Hot, moist and sweaty
Rapid is the pace of our heartbeat
Breathing heavily
The dimension of our passion
Too great to measure
Deep gallivant
Finding hidden treasures
Multiple arrangements of our body and limbs
Erotic flicks

Sequence of images
Teeth, tongues and lips
Chest, nipples and breast
Stomach, navel and abs
Vagina, clitoris and ass
Testicles and genitals
Legs, knees and thighs
Feet, fingers and nails
Our urge to gratify
As we utter impulsively
Oh so magnetic

PROVE IT

We are all the same
Made from the same elements
Water
Blood
Soul
Spirit
Energy
Bones
Flesh
Body
Etc...

The same senses
Smelling
Hearing
Seeing
Touching
Tasting

We have the same desires to
Eat
Drink
Sleep
Live
Love

Make love
Etc...

The same emotions
Joy
Passion
Happiness
Grief
Anger
Compassion
Etc...

The list can go on and on
If you know any difference
Besides our various shades
Dialect, culture or faith
Please let me in on the secret

Random Thinking

What is this world coming to?

An end

So I've been told

And today

I finally have seen some of the signs unfold

Like sinners judging sinners

As if one is greater than

Or less than the other.

Words don't hurt

But that's a lie

Harsh words and broken expectations

Can cut like a knife

Seasons change

As it should

And pain is just as strange

As when

The sun meets the rain.

Order is divine

And so is the cycle of life

The mind stores thoughts

Like love holds in the heart.

If boots are made for walking

And that's what they must do

Then why when your down

They stop walking

To stay and stomp on you.

These thoughts of mine are random

But at once they enter my mind

Like how a person with perfect vision

Can be so blind

To what is right before their eyes

Or shall I say

Under their nose.

It's human nature I suppose

To question the certain

And except the guess

There is no rhyme or reason

To the random thoughts

That lay upon my chest.

Forbidden Fruit

It seemed as if the instantly turned friends
Was just the lonely speaking again
When the heart yearns no more
The instantly turned friendship ends
Too afraid to face the reasons
If there is one
Every face has a season
And you finally shaded in one
You rather cut your bond loose
And hide from the truth
Shown by the spoken
Or shall I say the written
Never lend your friendship to the forbidden
Maybe a phase
Maybe a trip
Maybe it's AM
Or maybe it's your inside guilt
Whichever the case
You lost a confidant

Poetically Yours,

AM

Shh ...

In the light I'm hidden
In the night I'm seen
Unnoticed as I reflect
Shadowing your scene
In the fire I make flame
Acknowledge my body
Ignore my name
If I'm loved it's seldom seen
But filled with light is who I be
When thinking of me
Blank your mind goes
Keep the public in the dark
Better when no one else knows
Close your eyes and I'm the sight
Not clear in understanding
Total absence of light
Keeping the world's eyes masked
Is the only way they'll see
The dark beauty entity

MI CASA ES SU CASA

This night is for you
Let the stress from the week disappear
Let relaxation be here
This night is for you
Your simplest wish is my command
Your wildest dream is my thought out plan
This night is for you
Eat my food and drink my wine
Let the beautiful you completely shine
This night is for you
My duty for you this night is perfection
Your smiling face ... no exception
Mi Casa Es Su Casa

Making Up Feels So Good

I was still upset
When he smiled at me with his puppy dog eyes
Still apologizing about the night before
Brushing back my hair
Kissing me
Ignoring my attempts to push him away
Pulling me closer to him
Until his nose touched mine
Using his flirty ways
Getting me to smile was his okay
To distribute more kisses
To my forehead, my nose, my cheeks and my lips
I closed my eyes and gave into the sensation
Forgiving his mistake
When I should have given him a citation
For his violation
But our breakup makeup
Sends a better vibration up my spine

INSTINCT REACTS

Flirting with our eyes

Instinct reacts

Rude boy

Good girl

Opposites attract

The beauty marks on his

Face, neck, shoulders and chest

Need not be ignored

My minds eye explores

He's excited

Seeing my russet skin

His hands don't know where to begin

They start with running through my

Braided hair

He dared me to stare

To look upon him bare

His warm breath weakens me

As he

Kisses and bite my structured jaw bone

Then slightly he moans

He takes his hand and embrace my breast

My nipples harden

A mere reaction to his caress

I'm excited

Seeing his dark skin glisten

Dripping wet from sweat

In the middle of our ecstasy

My hands cuff his ears

Just as our eyes met

Again love is proved to be unbiased

Poetic Intercourse

Warm was my body when you felt my heartbeat
As we fought our resistance between the sheets
Sensually completely your turning me on
With your timing of ignition relative to our position
Tell me, how does it feel to desire my sex appeal?
Does your mind open
In the mental-physical allurement?
Undressing me with your eyes
As you watch me remove my undergarments
Exercising your leadership
When penetrating my source
Overwhelming is the feel in our poetic intercourse
Our love faces alone is as much as a turn on
As the act itself
Tell me, how does it feel in the center of our desires?
Cold and hot winds of our breath blows
As we make and unmake in passion
Intensity grows
Hotter, wetter and bolder
So much so, I bury my head into your shoulder
Not stopping the love or the feeling to entice
As you loved my body ... I loved your soul
Tantalizing my source with such a quiet force
Tasty is the feel in our poetic intercourse

LETTING GO

You damaged our connection
By showing less consideration
Acting as if you don't give a damn
Ignoring the fact that you love who I am
Being selfish with
Your love
Your reasoning
And your emotions
When knowing all along
That I had you open
Let me in on the inside secret
I'm known for keeping them well
And although our love didn't sail
You felt my flow
So act like you know
By letting love
Letting destiny
Or
By letting go

Reality

Love is what love feels

And if no one loves you back

Is it not real?

Crossed paths of mixed up people

Looking but not finding

Searching for a trial that is ever winding

When you finally stop

Running in circles

You'll see me

Waiting for the day

Together we will be free

What the soul longs for

The mind makes a way

Fiction is then banished

Reality is here to stay

Mind Games

Entering into a game
Without knowledge of the regulations
Agreeing to play fair in this relationship
Strapping on my mental belt
As I ride through his mental trip
Mind games the name
But only he knows the title
I'm playing with my heart
Because I was misled from the start
After months of participation
I developed a strategy
Now I'm moving forward
As I push him behind me
I'm feeling more aware
But there are missing clues
So I take some time to examine his rules
After decoding the codes
I'm now playing in expert mode
Now I'm in access of his mental grief
Leaving him stuck and stunned in disbelief

REFLECTION

In a world so aloof and confused
Lies a soul misused
Wanting to be free
Needing to be me
Curious of what people might say
As I remove my mask layer by lay
One after another my persona becomes real
With feelings of emotions
I remember how to feel
My heart is aching of words and thoughts
People think and say
Still I live my life
Day by day
I want to see what the still water sees
So I turn to the sea and stare at my
Reflection
Wondering if that is me
Or a speculation of whom I want to be
Then I look down into the sea again
And just see me
A Black American Queen

A Beautiful Disaster

A shooting star that shot too far

An innocent girl with a broken heart

A vision lost in the making

Held captive by love she's missing

Her void inside

From it

She runs … she hides

Scarred from the bruises

Sick from the tides

Caught up in a wave of lies

So genuine her love runs deep

All she want

Is someone to keep … to be kept

Someone to hold … to be held

To be free

Blinded by the seduction

And the words he said to please her

He created a beautiful disaster

BLIND MY EYES SO I CAN LOVE

Many suns, many moons and many roads

I have traveled

Found and lost love on the way

Many risks I have taken

Chancing consequence to face

Or rewards to profit

There's an effect to every cause

Frustration blocks builds a wall

Many hearts and many truths

Have unraveled

Leading me astray

Outer and inner scars

Have developed

Because in love I put my faith

Now today

I'm cynical to trust

Unless his heart has been kissed by the sun

Leaving his love blinding me by its rays

ADVICE TO YOUNG LOVES

During the middle of June

I became the bride and he the groom

Around high noon I walked down an aisle

As a live orchestra

Played the traditional wedding tune

My breast and neck fumed of Eau de Parfum

Something old, something new

Something borrowed, something blue

Were all apart of my costume

The day was as priceless as a family's heirloom

Each of our family members and friends

Witnessed our love in its full bloom

"Together Forever" we vowed to assume

Two years later

After our baby boomed from my womb

We found ourselves in a courtroom

Trying to convince a judge

That we've simply consumed too much too soon

So my advice to young loves

You must know what love is

To know when love is real

Before jumping the broom

DEFINED BY RULES

Rules, Rules, Rules

Why do we allow ourselves to be defined by rules?

Are there any exceptions

How can we lower our feelings

Without lowering our affection?

We have a commodity of exchanges

An agreement ... an arrangement

This is true ... but now

You want more from me and

You want to give me more of you

It isn't you ... it's me

Not an excuse to refuse your nearness

Or to keep things at a distance

Now I'm pushing you away

Things are going great

If this is true

Why should I choose my words more carefully?

I'm not here to deceive

Just speaking what I believe

At the moment

Can't we just live

By the moment, for the moment, and in the moment

Without defining rules?

Shaded Faces

Out of all the people Lord
You test my faith
Attracting my eyes to a man
Of a different land
Never say never
I thought I was too clever to fall
Into this trap called
Real love
That hunts us
My first thought
Oh my God!
I want this man but
He's foreign! He's foreign!
Will my parents understand
That I fell in love at first sight
We're all the same
The conditioned thoughts in my mind
I tried to change
Realizing our differences
And loving him just the same

POWER PLAY

Exercising our influence with seduction
Instinctive to us both
Eyes contact
Emotions react
Your lips on my lips
Merge wills and passion
I bite your collarbone
You kiss my shoulder blade
Your clothes drop to the floor
This is how the prestigious play
I expose expanses of skin
Your nature increase
Intensifying our determination to release
Inhaling my scent
Stimulates your intent
Your body pressed on my body
Your bulging to the occasion
I accept your physical invasion
Your warm tongue rhythm
Lead to my persuasion
What an irresistible motive
Intensifying our lust
This power play is between us
Seduction is a war of strategy

So to further the fascination

I let you watch my manual stimulation

As your body palpitate

Your whispers of moans are sexy

Telling me how good I feel

And how you can't live without me

Your velocity quickens

My neck stretches in pleasure

Our bodies quiver

And we liberate

BLIND IS LOVE

A prejudice correction has been made

When my affection

Went in a different direction

It was placed upon a man

Of a much lighter complexion

Our connection

Bypassed my protected conception

As I excepted his invitation

Now I'm convinced

Love is colorless

Unscramble Me

I'll verbally key into your imagination
And mentally unlock your mental
Opening dimensional sounds and mind
Lyrically guiding you into a rhyme of shadows
With blind folds ... I'll slip you into a darkness
Of an artist type of flow - I echo
Off (off) the (the) top (top) of (of)
Mount (Mount) Everest (Everest)
Alone at the top where it's
Dark and the sun cannot be seen
I gleam through the night like an infra red beam
Just when it seemed ... all things were green
All hidden objects were being seen
Even on the other side
I smoke grass until my eyes bleed
You'll lose blood internally
Trying to battle me poetically
I'm a well spoken blessing ... unwritten
Although some sound to seem
Bigger, better or worst
They exaggerate in every line they state in verse
Unscramble me
This is my mind on rhymes

Mind Gamez

From lack of respect
A love triangle formed
Telling my best friend
You wanted her mind, body and soul
Convincing her to open up and to let her hair blow
Pampering her to relax
Once you got her in the sack
You tried to take the images you created
And the promises you vowed back
It's a little late for that
Her love is real
While you're playing with my best friends heart
There's missing cards you neglected to deal
Like the mistress out of town
You obviously didn't care too much for
When you and my best friend
Went rolling on the floor
So if my best friend wants to question you
Or leave you
She has every right to
Because your love was never true
Screw you hoodwink

DOES HE KNOW HIM?

The face that everyone else may see
Doesn't describe the true he
Driving the nicest cars
Hanging out late in bars
Telling a lady to page him late night
Lying to wifey just to avoid a fight
Then he brag to his boys that his game is tight
But deep in his soul he know it's not right
However being cool
Is his way of being accepted
He don't care that his true self is rejected
His true wants neglected
As long as he do what his friends expected
Because it seems his life is their life
And he's being directed
It's all part of the game as long as his name rings
He's the man that he can't stand
Because yesterday's misery
Is tomorrow's pain
Being but not seeing
Knowing the outcome but not fleeing
He keep asking himself will he ever be free
It's doubtful when him don't even know the real he

GREY HOUND BUS

My first ride on the grey hound bus
Was during the middle of August
My friend and I packed almost everything we owned
We packed snacks and Heineken
To relax us on the road
Luckily we got two seats in the same row
So we were able to sit together
We saw beautiful rivers and acres of orange trees
We saw horses and cows
From beautiful mountain tops
We drove through quiet towns
And through noisy cities
We saw people rafting in lakes
For three days we witnessed such a
Remarkable scenery
As we past through each state
Our memories of this trip is great
However
We both agreed to travel by airplane
For our next trip

There Is No End

All together ... destine souls
It is a day of poor weather
Music cranks ... notes flatly blend
A still air
File in ranks and boys off to war
Send caskets to unbending places
Caskets unyielding a face
Friends
Ends
Friends dressed in red, white and blue
And forever tortured
A soul
Oh ... fighting war
Music to soothe the soul ... sacrifice more
Men move on the kill
Yes souls kill
Souls kill flesh and vessel
Without redemption
I wrestle
A score for hell
You see
You don't die in hell
It's that little tie
That captures torture
Forever

Israel

A land of milk and honey
But what lies beneath the grain
For His bread has no yeast
Yet leaven it grows
We are mankind
Born to His hills
Is the land His
Is the water
Is the fig tree holy to her
Holy mother
His hills
Sort of like footsteps
Has the shadow of God been there all along?
Is this the question
Or the answer
Or the purpose?
My foot slips on this sand
A movement that startled a weight of grain
That caught me off balance
Yet from the grain beneath I am His
The foundation of the world
FAITH

ROUTINE

I knew it was love

When he looked upon me with such gaze

His touch gave such comfort

He kissed me

As if he wanted to savor every taste of my

Tongue and saliva

He inhaled my aroma

As if he wanted to remember my scent forever

He looked upon me

As if he were mentally taking pictures of

My every expression

He except me as I am

We share much moments

We enjoy each others company

Making each other smile

Became routine

Dear Tonka

LOVE

Love yourself

Respect yourself

Trust your instincts

Follow your dreams

Be free from fear

Put nothing on hold

Pick your friends wisely

Keep your head up

Make eye contact

Stay focused

Never ever try drugs

Cleanliness is next to Godliness

Lead by example

Do your best

If fallen ... get up ... try again

Fight for what you believe in

Have a reason

Face responsibilities head on

Protect yourself by any means necessary

Be kind to animals

Eat healthy and exercise regularly

Take risk

Travel

Smell flowers and learn their names

Take caution

Live honestly

Encourage others

Knowledge is power

Meditate

Believe

Read

Invest

Seek

Give to someone in need

Don't believe everything you hear or see

Use wisdom

Work hard

Take it easy

Take control

Take lots & lots & lots of pictures

Smile and

Laugh as often as possible

Travion, I salute you, I admire and honor your greatness;
I love you for all that you are.
Love Your Mother, Asia Marie Jackson

Who Am I?

I'm God's child
An unsolved mystery
An untold story
A love song that lingers in your mind
A vision of beauty
An amazing person
A loving mother
An encouraging sister
A loyal daughter
A devoted best friend
Who am I?
I'm refreshing
A breath of fresh air
A vision in a poets dream
A warm embrace
I'm the jazz of a song
I'm energy
I'm intuition
I'm laughter
Who am I?
I'm unfrozen
And everyone knows it including me

SCORPIO

You express yourself well
And have a flair for the written word
You subscribe to the maxim
"If its worth doing its worth doing it well"
You are haughty but justly so
You rank high with your society
You social butterfly
You like to plan for the future
Determination and willpower are your basic traits
You are imaginative where romance is concerned
You can be extremely secretive by nature
You can be a very trusted friend
Alternatively, you can be a most fearsome enemy
You love with fierce devotion
You are passionate with everything
You are exceptional, mysterious
And totally magnetic

FRAME OF MIND

It's my frame of mind
I'm on a cosmic journey
Trying to reach the other side
Trying to get high
It's my frame of mind
Filing all life stories
Trying to find the truth in lies
Trying to stay high
It's my frame of mind
To love not push aside
Together stand not divide
If we try
We will reach limits beyond the sky
It's my frame of mind
Trying to see through love that's blind
Trying to keep my high
When we start this new beginning
That's when life will have its full meaning
If we try
We will reach limits beyond the sky
Together we'll stay high

Fluttering Beauty

I remember the first time my son caught a
Monarch butterfly
Its wings featured a
Beautiful black and orange pattern
The capture was an amazing sight to see
He stood amongst the flowers
Patiently watching
The butterfly flutter through the garden
Keeping his eyes on the fluttering beauty
Waiting for it to hold still

He moved in on the butterfly
Swiftly yet calmly and determined
As a lion moves in on its prey
Once he was close enough
He steadied his hand
Capturing the fluttering beauty by its wings
He then bought the butterfly to eye level
And looked on it a brief moment
"I got it!"

Realizing what he had done
He ran to me with the monarch in hand
And a look of accomplishment in his eyes

He showed me that
He did
Indeed
Catch the fluttering beauty by its wings

Then after giving it another brief stare
He released the fluttering beauty
Back into the open space above the garden

At that moment
I knew
That he now knew
The great feeling accomplishing a goal
Can give a man

God Made Me Free

When God made the oceans and the seas
He gave them boundaries
So they would not over flood the earth
When God created me
He gave no boundaries
God made me free
Let it be ... let it be
God made the stars to illuminate the night
God made me also a very bright and shining light
But you pretend not to see
Stop and take a look at me
I am the representation
Of every dark skin person you will ever see
And God has placed such an excellent spirit
Inside of me
I shall exceed all limits
Given me by society
God placed me in a home
Where the air was clean to breath
Free from injustice, degradation and immorality
In my home all were free to enjoy life
The way God planned it to be
I was stolen from my home
The country of my birth

And forced to work for people that claimed
I had no worth
I've been whipped, I've been hung
I've been cheated, I've been chained
Yet of these things
I am not ashamed
Because it happened during my season of rain
But now the dark clouds have now been
Rolled away
And for me it is a brand new day
Today I am a doctor, a lawyer
A judge, a school teacher, a business owner
And a Presidential Candidate
I am all the things I have ever hoped to be
Because God has given me the victory
God made me free
Let it be … let it be

By, Orange Arie

ME BEING ME

The way I used to live my life
Definitely me being me
In those days.
Although I was influenced by
Society and my surroundings
Me being me never changed
After sitting through years
Of my mothers lectures and molding
After years of education
Good and bad relationships.
After bearing a life
Knowing my blood runs through his veins
And after all the laughter, hurt and pain
After the heartaches, headaches and tough breaks
After church Sundays
Family influence
Old, new, distant, close and loving friends
The way I live my life today
Definitely me being me
In these days.
Please don't mistake
Because I speak a different speech
Think a different thought
That the old me can't be reclaimed

I'm a beautiful soft-spoken woman
With the same name
Lively, humble, caring and smart
Yet very hard to tame.
So what I'm trying to say is
That I'm not trying to say or be anything
I'm just me being me
Saying, doing and being
Exactly what I meant to say, do and be.
So stop lurking to identify what you think is
Between the lines
And just read the lines you see
And you'll find that the old, new and future me
Makes me the same person that I am … Asia

www.ingramcontent.com/pod-product-compliance
Lightning Source LLC
LaVergne TN
LVHW041630070426
835507LV00008B/536